SCRYING

A Feminine Mode of Divination

Also by Raymond A. Moody

Life After Life

Reflections on Life After Life

Laugh After Laugh

Elvis After Life

The Light Beyond

Coming Back

Reunions

To the Tunnel and Beyond

SCRYING

A FEMININE MODE OF DIVINATION

Raymond A Moody, Jr., Ph.D., M.D.

R. Bemis Publishing, Ltd.
Marietta, Georgia 30007

SCRYING:
A Feminine Mode of Divination

Copyright 1995, by Raymond A. Moody, Jr.,
Ph.D., M.D.

ISBN: 0-89176-999-4

Cover concept by David Productions
Cover design by Penstroke Graphics; Atlanta, GA
Graphic design and graphics by
Penstroke Graphics; Atlanta, GA

Printed in the United States of America

First Printing: November, 1995

R. Bemis Publishing, Ltd.
P.O. Box 71088
Marietta, Georgia 30007

About the Author

Raymond A. Moody, Jr., Ph.D., M.D., is a world-renowned scholar and researcher, and the leading authority on the near death experience, as well as the author of nine books, including the best-selling *Life After Life* (10 million copies sold to date) and numerous articles for professional and academic journals.

Dr. Moody was born in Poterdale, GA, and received a Bachelor of Arts, with honors in philosophy, a Master of Arts in philosophy, and a Ph.D. in philosophy from the University of Virginia, and earned a Medical Doctor degree at the Medical College of Georgia. Moody has taught philosophy at the University of Virginia and East Carolina University; psychology at West Georgia College, and has been a practicing psychiatrist. Additionally, Moody has spoken to groups and scholars in both the US and Europe, and has received numerous awards for his contributions in the field of paranormal research.

Dr. Moody currently serves as a Director of Special Programs for the Parapsychological Service Institute, is an Associate Editor of *The Journal of Near Death Studies*, and is the director of a parapsychological research facility in rural Alabama, where he resides with his wife Cheryl.

ACKNOWLEDGMENTS

Most of all, it is my students at West Georgia College whom I need to thank. They listened patiently as I was formulating my ideas about scrying and cheerfully participated in demonstrations of crystal gazing. My colleagues Dr. William Roll, who in 1986 first introduced me to the subject of scrying, and Dr. Mike Arons, who encouraged me in my investigations into this and other curiosities of the mind, also played a major role in this book.

Over a period of several years, the Parapsychological Services Institute provided me with a forum at numerous conferences and workshops to develop these thoughts. Without their cooperation, there is no doubt that this monograph would never have been written.

My friend Bill Liggin also expressed interest in this subject at an early stage of my research, and I appreciate his encouragement and support. Grant Brown assisted by preparing brochures for the Institute of Scrying and Dream Incubation, and Joyce Johnson took charge of addressing and mailing them and helped in many ways in an advisory capacity.

Finally, I want to thank Royce Bemis, the publisher of R. Bemis Publishing, Ltd., and Mockingbird Books, and the publisher of the hardback edition of *Life After Life*, who has worked with me carefully over a long period of time to help ensure the publication of this work. His humor and dedication have been unfailing.

PROLEGOMENA

This book is intended to be read in the context of having already read two earlier scholarly volumes which deal—though not solely—with the subject of scrying. They are:

Crystal Gazing: Its History and Practice, with a Discussion of the Evidence for Telepathic Scrying. Copyright 1905. By Northcote W. Thomas; with an Introduction by Andrew Lang.

Crystal Gazing: A Study in the History, Distribution, Theory and Practice of Scrying. Copyright 1924. By Theodore Besterman.

Both are now out of print. However, *Crystal Gazing,* as well as other works in this genre, will be reprinted by R. Bemis Publishing, Ltd. in the near future.

With the publication of *Scrying: A Feminine Mode Of Divination,* I hope to awaken the interest of a community of scholars to the subject of scrying, one of the many odd phenomena of the mind, which have, by and large, escaped serious scrutiny.

Scrying is the practice of interpreting visions, seen or allegedly seen, in the optical clear depth of a speculum whose purpose is that of divination.

Scrying is of great interest for a number of reasons, not the least of which is that it has become the object of scholarly taboos; not discussed or investigated, but held to ridicule. Indeed, it has been relegated to the realm(s) of the cartoonist. Curiously, the grounds for the establishment of this taboo seem to be related to the fact that scrying has come to be a publicly promulgated archetype of superstition, one of a tableau of images: a black cat silhouetted against the moon; the number thirteen; a gypsy and her crystal ball; a rabbit's foot; a ladder propped against a wall. So, scholarship's trepidation on the matter seems to be a fuzzily defined fear, or guilt by association.

Though this book will be of interest to the general reader, I also am attempting, through its publication, to enlist a number of scholars from various fields to join in a collective and cooperative adventure: a unique participant-observer study (loosely defined) of scrying; a systematic but pre-scientific study.

I propose an invitation to those who will participate: Let us see what can happen if we disavow the fear of inquiry and plunge ahead to attempt what we are told should not be done, and in a way in which we are told we should not do it. Let us see what the outcomes can be of simply, and self-consciously, breaking a scholarly taboo.

Scrying: A Feminine Mode of Divination is intended to be a manual for co-investigators in this project. For this reason the book is written in such a way as to arouse curiosity, to provoke discussion, and to generate questions about scrying rather than simply to provide information.

This project is being undertaken under the auspices of the Institute of Scrying and Dream Incubation, an institution that is dedicated to resurrecting, systematically studying, and preserving knowledge about those ancient methods of divination which employ techniques of inducing visionary states: scrying (by use of crystal gazing), dream incubation, catoptromancy (by use of mirror gazing), capnomancy (by use of smoke gazing), and related phenomena, including hypnagogic experiences and lucid dreaming.

The mode of the current study will be non-parapsychological. It has become all too obvious that studying scrying from the perspective of trying to find concrete evidence of foreknowledge, or clairvoyance, has led nowhere.

Therefore, let us proceed without invoking beliefs about the occurrence of paranormal phenomena. Let us, in fact, studiously avoid any attempt to discover or to prove the paranormal. Rather, let us endeavor to become familiar with scrying as a curiosity of human culture, an antique of human consciousness, an artifact, perhaps, from the worlds of persons living long, long ago.

Although this systematic study will not be a parapsychological (nor even a properly scientific) one, it will not be a debunking one either. And, in some aspects, it will be an experiential one.

So I offer the reader a beginning in the way of an exercise, a method of evoking visions of one's own. Although firsthand experiences of crystal visions, or even of crystal gazing, are by no means necessary for the scholarly study of scrying, both (or either) can very definitely enrich such study.

The main thing, after all, is to relax. The subject of this work is of intrinsic interest, quite apart from one's own personal visions.

Raymond A. Moody, Jr., M.D., Ph.D.

PART I.
SCRYING: AN ANTIQUE PROFESSION

CHAPTER 1

AN INTRODUCTION TO SCRYING

Scrying: A Feminine Mode of Divination is the result of an extended attempt to think clearly and dispassionately about an extraordinary, antique profession, which has in our times achieved the status of an icon. This is the trade of the *scryer*, the diviner who claims (or pretends) to discover occult knowledge for her clients by interpreting visions seen in a crystal ball. I say "her," advisedly, because the public image of the scryer is that of a female: a dark woman, often a gypsy, staring into a crystal ball and professing to foretell the future.

Here, however—as we shall later see—are the many ways the familiar image of *scrying* is quite misleading. In this book I propose to demythologize scrying so as to reveal what, if anything, one can reasonably believe about this strange profession, and what about it one can reasonably reject.

We will begin, in Chapter 2, by setting out a thorough definition of scrying in terms of certain core concepts, or features, which are inexorably linked to scrying in the public perception. Thereafter, we will use this definition of scrying to illuminate a number of related or derivative issues, which are as follows.

In Chapter 3 we will illustrate why it is impossible to speak meaningfully of a history of scrying. We shall then set up a novel framework which will allow for a coherent exposition of the facts about scrying which cannot plausibly be recounted in the form of an historical narrative.

In Chapter 4 we will explore three areas of social concern—fringe professions, illegality, and superstition and the paranormal—insofar as they are closely interrelated with the public image of scrying. In so doing, we will show how our multidimensional definition of scrying sheds light on each of the four parts of this book.

In Chapter 5, I will recount a unique participant-observer exercise which I conducted in order to gain personal insight into the inner and outer workings of this trade. Concomitantly, I will make some remarks about divination and fringe professions in general which, hopefully, will be enlightening.

Finally, in Chapter 6 I will use our multidimensional definition and all that we have learned from this part to demonstrate and to diagnose how the public image of scrying generates obfuscating, unnecessary dilemmas and difficulties for science, for scholarship, and for society as a whole.

In closing, I will show how, properly considered and employed, our definition enables us to see what is sense and what is nonsense with respect to scrying. Hopefully we will thereby liberate scholars to investigate certain demonstrably real phenomena of the mental, and possibly even spiritual, life which, heretofore, have for too long been regarded as off-limits for serious study.

We will now turn to the task of analyzing this complex phenomenon/image/activity into its component features and aspects. Let us begin.

CHAPTER 2

A MULTIDIMENSIONAL DEFINITION
OF SCRYING

Upon analysis, the image one has of scrying and of the scryer is not simple, but complex. In our minds' eye we envision not a single entity but a scene: a woman sits, usually in an exotic dress, in a small room or tent. On a table before her sits a crystal ball. She dramatically waves her hand(s) over the ball, as she appears to gaze into the far distance. Opposite her at the table waits an apprehensive and credulous client, who anxiously anticipates her pronouncements on what the future will bring.

In this one description we have touched upon seven distinct aspects, of scrying: the term "scry," the speculum, crystal visions, ritual, the feminine, and relationship divination. Now let's analyze them.

THE TERM "SCRY." The verb "to scry", and hence the derivative words "scrying" and "scryer," are abbreviated forms of the verb "to descry." The word was adopted into English from French in the thirteenth century, in the Middle English word "descrien."

It is plain that the word relates to knowledge and to the acquisition thereof. It means "to discern," "to notice," "to detect," "to perceive," even "to discover," and carries the added implication of that which is "discerned, discovered, etc.," by looking carefully.

Clearly, this word is one which would be of great interest to the epistemologist. Proponents of the ordinary language school of analytic philosophy would no doubt note that it somehow entails a kind of *success* at knowing or coming to know. If one says, "I discerned Jane way down there in the valley," or "I detected a weakness in your argument," or "I discovered a new enzyme in the liver," one is making a claim to *truth*. That is, one is by implication claiming as a minimum that it is *true* Jane was way down there in the valley, that it is *true* there is a weakness in the argument, that it is *true* there exists such-and-such, a previously unknown enzyme in the liver.

This implication is central to the meaning of the term and is revealed by the way in which conventional linguistic usage effectively insulates the integrity of the words' implication of truth from human lapses or mistakes. For if, later, it turns out that what one said in claiming to "descry, to discern, to detect, to discover" was *untrue*—that Jane was not, in fact, in the valley at that time; the argument was sound after all; that the supposed new enzyme was just a contaminant—then something quite magical happens. Under these circumstances the properly trained speaker says, *not* "I discerned Jane down in the valley," but "it turned out not to be her but her sister Sally;" *not* "I detected a weakness in your argument," but "your argument turned out to be sound;" *not* "I discovered a new enzyme in the liver" but "it turned out that the supposed new enzyme was just a contaminant;" but, rather, "I thought (or mistakenly believed, etc.) that I discerned Jane...but it turned out..., etc."; "I *thought* I detected..., etc."; or *"thought* I discovered..., etc."

6

Such considerations are more than semantics. They make it manifest that one is dealing here with a mode of knowing or of coming to know.

SPECULUM. Of necessity, it seems, scrying must be done with a speculum of some sort. In the standard version of the icon—at least in our society—this instrument is a crystal ball. However, this obscures the fact, not widely known, that a host of substances, artifacts, objects, or surfaces have been used for this activity. What they all must have in common is that they have a reflective quality, a sort of transparency and clarity through and into which the scryer can peer as if at a great distance.

In point of fact, different varieties of scrying are named in accordance with the nature of the speculum employed. Hence,

When the speculum employed is a:	Then the activity is called:
crystal ball	crystallomancy
sword blade	macharomancy
fingernail or thumbnail	onchyomancy
mirror	catoptromancy
bowl of liquid	lecanomancy
and so on.	

CRYSTAL VISIONS. It is assumed that the scryer sees, or at least pretends to see, visions in the depths of the speculum. That certain individuals do see visions—specifically, hypnagogic images—when gazing into a transparent or reflective surface is a well-established fact that can be regarded as an item of psychological knowledge. However, the relation between the profession of scrying and crystal visions is by no means simple or straightforward.

In its pure form scrying is a way of using and interpreting visions. One can assume that some scryers do see visions when peering into their speculums. However, D.H. Rawcliffe asserts in his book *Occult and Supernatural Phenomenon* that there is a "class of 'scryer' [who] never sees anything in his crystal. He is a charlatan pure and simple."

What Rawcliffe asserts as a matter of principle, I have directly observed.

I went incognito to the makeshift studio of one of these pretenders in order to scrutinize his technique. The seer was a middle-aged gentleman dressed neatly in a blue business suit. His manner was one of firm self-assurance. His glass "crystal" ball was cradled in a flashy metal tripod which rested on a bare table top, and the lights in the room were intensely bright.

During our session the scryer made an unconvincing and, I sensed, a somewhat self-conscious pretense of looking not into but rather at the glass ball. I believe that if I had confronted him at this time with the information that I was a professor of psychology, a non-occultist, and that to my professional knowledge certain individuals do in fact see visions when gazing into a clear depth, he would have been every bit as surprised as was I a year before when I had first learned that fact.

RITUAL. When reflecting on folk beliefs regarding scrying and perusing what literature exists on the subject, one gains the impression that the activity is enshrouded in a fog of ritualistic practices. The commonly known ones are that the client must first "cross the prophet's palm with silver" (though most accept paper now), and that the seer or seeress must wave his or her hands mysteriously over the crystal before beginning. There are, however, a host of other rituals.

The following examples are a few, which I have culled from my reading on the subject:

- The scryer must purchase his own crystal, paying the price which the seller asks.

- The scryer must cleanse the crystal prior to each scry with, for example, vinegar or spring water.

- The scryer must begin each session with a prayer, or exorcism, to keep away evil spirits.

- No one except the scryer is to be allowed to touch the crystal.

- The scryer is to be dressed in exotic garb.

These represent the aspect of scrying that is often referred to as "mumbo-jumbo." In the public mind, bizarre ritual is inexorably linked to the practice of scrying.

THE FEMININE. In our society, in contemporary times, one thinks of the scryer as a woman, as a simple inspection of the conventional icon will reveal. Historically, however, nothing could be further from the truth: Nostradamus, the Aztec priests, and the chief oracle of Tibet are among the many glaring exceptions. On a deeper level, the popular conception has much to recommend it.

9

One thinks of receptivity as a feminine trait, and this is precisely the state of mind which is evocative of hypnagogic imagery. So there is good reason to think of scrying as a specifically *female mode of divination.*

RELATIONSHIP. In principle and of necessity, the scryer must have clients, for otherwise there could not be such a profession. That is, scrying of necessity involves a human relationship: that which subsists between the scryer and the person supposedly served. On occasion a third party is introduced into the situation. In earlier times, scryers chose to employ someone—typically a young child —to do the crystal gazing. This surrogate crystal gazer, best described as a kind of psychic technician, would report the vision(s) to the scryer, who, in turn, would interpret the vision(s) on behalf of the client. This fact makes it plain that one does not have to be a crystal gazer in order to be a scryer.

It is this supposed power, or ability, to interpret crystal visions which is the hallmark of scrying, or the presumed opinion that the scryer has a paranormal talent—a psychic gift, as it were—which is possessed by only a few of us. It is the possession of this gift which, in effect, gives the scryer her authority in relationship to the client. For she is regarded as having this ability, through her power of interpretation, to uncover hidden, or occult, knowledge.

DIVINATION. Divination is, by definition, the practice, or process, of foretelling the future or discovering hidden knowledge by supernatural or occult means.

Let us look at the ends which scrying as a form of divination has in fact served. They are four:

10

• First, the scryer purports to pierce the veil of futurity, to peer into a time yet to come and to discover what lurks there.

• Secondly, scrying has been used in attempts to see what is transpiring at present at a great distance, beyond the reach of the human senses. It was used in this way, for example, by the rulers of huge countries in order to determine what was happening in distant corners of their territory.

• Thirdly, scryers sometimes have been consulted for assistance in locating lost or misplaced objects. The specularii of medieval times, for example, appear to have specialized in this task.

• Fourthly, scrying was used for criminal detection, for instance,finding out who stole the jewels or committed the murder. Typically, the scryer would report seeing the figure or face of the guilty party in his speculum. The client would then infer the identity of the offender from his descriptions.

We now have completed our multidimensional definition of scrying, and it should be obvious that the seven features, or elements, of scrying which have been identified are interconnecting and mutually supporting. The fact that crystal visions, being hypnagogic phenomena, require the gazer to be relaxed and receptive may, as we have already seen, helps us to understand why scrying is thought of as a specifically feminine form of divination. The fact that the word "scrying" implies that truth is being discovered helps us understand how the process is thought of as a form of divination.

The relationship between scryer and client depends upon the assumption that the scryer has a peculiar type of gift, one which makes divination possible. It is obvious that certain rituals surrounding scrying are intended to establish, and to reinforce, the relationship between the scryer and the client.

Hence, we are ready to move on to our next task: the perplexities surrounding the notion of a history of scrying.

CHAPTER 3

THE NON-HISTORY OF SCRYING

It was my original intention to write a history of scrying, but in attempting to do so I discovered certain insurmountable difficulties which have been, in themselves, revelatory of the nature of this strange and romantic profession. The first thing one finds when researching this topic is that there is a dearth of scholarly material on the subject. I was unable to find even a single volume on scrying which has any plausible claim to being scholarly. The subject is discussed, along with other topics, in a 1905 book entitled *CRYSTAL GAZING*, written by the English scholar Northcote Thomas. However, the author is so obsessed by the paranormal that he fails to make any serious attempt to distinguish between the psychological phenomenon of crystal visions and that specific use of them for the purpose of divination which constitutes scrying.

Thomas aspires to treat the subject historically, but it is plain that his effort is a failure. The "historical" part of his book is divided into sections, designated "New World," "Asia," "Malayas," "India," "Africa," "Romans," "Italy," "England," and so on, which consist simply of anecdotes about practices which pertain to those specific localities or cultures.

But Thomas's failure to construct a satisfactory history of the subject by no means results entirely from his own shortcomings. In fact, his failure stems, at least as much, from the overall impossibility of writing a unified historical narrative on the subject of scrying. There is no continuous strand of development of this profession weaving through time and crossing through numerous cultures, knitting them together as there is, for example, in the case of science, medicine, or even, to a much lesser degree, literature. Rather, with scrying there are only here-and-there fits and starts, a crazy quilt of independent emergence, flourishings and disappearances. Although Thomas calls what he has done an historical approach, it is patent that his approach is instead geographical and cultural.

However, the impossibility of casting Thomas's material into the form of historical narrative by no means entails that the material itself is not worthwhile. In fact, the temporally and geographically scattered episodes which he compiles are of intrinsic interest and are potentially helpful in the task of constructing an overall analysis of the profession of scrying.

Accordingly, in my opinion, what is called for is a novel way of organizing such material as Thomas compiles which at once circumvents the objection that a coherent history of scrying is impossible and also provides for easy accessibility for purposes of scholarship. I propose that just such an indexing scheme can be derived from the multidimensional definition(s) of scrying by considering three elements of that definition (namely: speculum, relationship, and divination), and adding to it cultural, geographical and temporal designation.

To review: we already noted that (1) many types of speculums have been used for scrying; (2) some scryers do, and others do not, hire other persons, such as young children, actually to do the crystal gazing; and (3) divination has been performed for four ends: foretelling the future, seeing events taking place at a distance, criminal detection, and locating lost objects. Let us set up a classificatory scheme:

S means "type of speculum"

R1 means "scryer both sees and interprets visions"

R2 means "scryer interprets visions seen by a surrogate crystal gazer"

D1 means "fortune telling"

D2 means "seeing events transpiring at a distance"

D3 means "criminal detection"

D4 means "locating lost objects"

Coupling this with a simple temporal and cultural designation, one can simply and conveniently display all such information as is to be found in Thomas's "historical" accounts of scrying.

For example, it is known that (1) Aztec priests foretold the future and attempted to divine what was happening in remote outposts of the empire by gazing into obsidian mirrors; (2) the chief oracle of Tibet used a polished steel mirror to predict the future for the government ministers; (3) the *specularii* were traveling scryers in medieval Europe who used mirrors to locate lost objects and tell fortunes; (4) in India, diviners placed a drop of oil on the thumbnail of a child and interpreted the visions seen by the child in order to help their clients determine who had stolen their property and how to recover it; (5) "Andronicus Comnenus had recourse to a hydromantic divisor to discover his successor, whom he intended to dispose of by violent means at the first opportunity," (Thomas, p. 65) and so on.

15

One can capture the essence of each of these Thomas anecdotes, respectively, as follows:

(1) Aztec: pre-Columbian
S = *obsidian mirror*
R1
D1, **D2**

(2) Tibet: remote times into recent decades
S = *steel mirror*
R1
D1

(3) Europe: medieval period
S = *mirror*
R1
D1, **D4**

(4) India: up to nineteenth century
S = *oil on thumbnail*
R2
D3, **D4**

(5) Rome: antiquity
S = water
R1
D1

It should be clear that this method can be employed to encompass any, and all, anecdotes about specific occurrences of scrying in any particular cultural and temporal context. In adopting this scheme of presentation and recording of such material, however, we are moving away from the study of history and into the territory of the social sciences. This method is reminiscent more of anthropology and sociology than it is of history. Let us now go on to explore in depth certain aspects of the social dimension of scrying.

CHAPTER 4

SCRYING IN SOCIETY: THREE ASPECTS

During the course of several years' experience lecturing on scrying to undergraduate and graduate students of psychology, I came to realize that, like me, most of my students had first been exposed to the subject as an object of ridicule in the form of cartoon humor. I never found even a single student who had not previously heard of divination by crystal gazing.

I conducted an informal public opinion survey among these students during that time. The results revealed a pronounced tendency for persons in our society to think of scrying in terms of three dimensions of social concern: (1) illegality, (2) fringe professions, and (3) superstition and the paranormal. We will consider each of these in turn.

ILLEGALITY. People tend to think of scrying as being against the law, as in fact it is in some localities. In his book *Superstition and the Press*, Curtis MacDougall states that the New York Code of Criminal Procedure forbids fortune telling in order "to prevent the ignorant and the gullible as well as the curious from being ensnared by the guiles and fantasies of those who profess to be able to 'crystal gaze' as to the course of human events."

It is clear here that what is illegal is the use of crystal gazing to foretell the future (i.e., scrying) on behalf of someone else, a client. Consideration of the law makes it quite clear that it is divination which is forbidden, and not crystal gazing *per se*. It obviously would be an absurdity to attempt to ban crystal visions themselves, since they may occur spontaneously and in other context than that of divination.

FRINGE PROFESSIONS. Since long before the beginning of recorded history, humans beings have sought the help of practitioners of a host of fringe professions. These practitioners claim to possess a specialized knowledge and to be able to put that knowledge to use in such a way as to help their clients.

Professions tend to come and go over historical time, and many which were highly respected in earlier eras have dropped out of existence. In seventeenth century Europe, for example, it was an accepted belief among persons whose trade required public speaking—attorneys, ministers, and so on—that they must periodically consult a practitioner in order to get their foreheads blistered. This process, at that time, was believed to strengthen the voice and improve the ability to speak before the public. A century earlier, in Britain, "common prickers" traveled the countryside sticking pins in elderly women suspected of being witches. The pricker would insert the pin in a point on the woman's body, out of her sight, and if the woman flinched, she was exonerated of the charge. If she showed no evidence of pain, however, this was proof positive of her guilt. Many people were burned at the stake based on the testimony at trial of these strange technicians.

The rules and principles—if any be—which govern the origin and decline of professions are not set out or understood. We in the modern age tend to assume that it is the inexorable progress of science which drives this cycle of emergence and disappearance, but the psychologically informed will realize that point of view is naive. Far more likely causes are to be found among those fundamental wishes and weaknesses which have given birth to, and nourished, human folly, fashion, and fad.

In modern society, there exist professions the traditions and history of which go back for many centuries, in some cases thousand of years: scholarship and academe, science, medicine, the law, the clergy, and in some respects statesmanship. These accepted and established professions continue through long periods of time because they subserve basic and universal human needs. They maintain their authority through such methods as rigorous training programs for would-be initiates and through adherence to conventionally established methodologies and/or procedures (e.g. the scientific method) which have stood the test of time.

Alongside these accepted professions, there are various institutions which claim to be professions but whose claims are held, somehow, to be dubious by large segments of society. They are the fringe professions. Often, they originate as an idiosyncratic doctrine, or discovery, of an eccentric person, even a crank, who feels that he has discovered a truth heretofore unknown to science. This doctrine is then promulgated, often over long periods of time, by converts, who usually must continue the refrain typically enunciated by the founder of that science. As one surveys fringe professions, it is hard to avoid the impression that their practitioners, all too often, are persons who, for whatever reason, felt that to master the principles of a regular discipline would have been too difficult or too time consuming. They seem to want to share in the authority which they imagine to be vested in an established profession without having to subject themselves to the rigors of the training. Typically, their stock-in-trade is an authoritative pronouncement, which they assume as an interpersonal style rather than on the basis of study and science. They like to be called by a title—"Doctor" or "Professor" or whatever—which, again, they appropriate from established professions, but ultimately, only in a kind of pathetic imitation of what is, even in their own minds, "the real thing."

Accordingly, they tend to advance their cause through pseudo-scientific argumentation and by political pressure rather than by scientific means. Persons tend to support such a fringe profession out of good will—if it works.

The ultimate fate of fringe professions varies widely. Some of them, like common prickers and head blisterers, vanish over time as the fad dies. Some are incorporated into mainstream professions. As an example, osteopathy, over a period of time, rigorously improved its educational and training programs to the point that it became indistinguishable from conventional medicine, and the D.O. and M.D. degrees are now equivalent and interchangeable. (And, indeed, in this author's opinion, since osteopaths have a broader-based and more humanely-focused training, they have overtaken M.D.'s and now make the very best physicians.)

Quite a few fringe professions have split into conflicting or even hostile sects, the opposing parties separating themselves one from another over some tenet that is regarded as central. Fringe professions may maintain themselves over long periods of time by appealing to the public on a psychological rather than scientific basis. Fortune telling is a good example.

Clearly, it is in this fringe that scrying is to be found. Unlike many fringe professions, however, in which the practitioners often pay lip service to science, except when its findings impinge upon their inviolable central doctrine, scrying overtly acknowledges its involvement with the paranormal.

SUPERSTITION AND THE PARANORMAL. In the public mind, scrying has become synonymous with superstition, and it is invariably linked with the paranormal. But we are not too clear, if asked, exactly what about scrying is to be regarded as a superstition. The statement that scrying is a superstition is subject to two distinct interpretations:

A. The belief that the future may be divined by the interpretation of visions seen in a clear depth is a superstition.

B. The belief that visions can be seen in a clear depth is a superstition.

It is patently obvious that the two interpretations are different. In fact, while in my opinion and in that of many others A is quite correct, B is demonstrably false, since it is known that many persons do experience hypnagogic imagery when gazing into a crystal ball or other speculum.

Most people, when thinking about scrying, have no conscious awareness of the distinction between A and B, and, hence, are led into error. It is often through failure to make this distinction that people are drawn into paranormal beliefs and that scrying is identified with the paranormal.

In modern society, the paranormal itself is organized and conceptualized in the form of a fringe or pseudo-profession, *viz.* parapsychology. Its adherents think of parapsychology as a branch of science; how odd it is, though, that a science should exist which seems to have as its object establishing the reality of the very phenomena or forces which it presumes exist in order to study them.

If scrying can be thought of as an applied science, then parapsychology is to be regarded as the theoretical and experimental science. In relation to scrying, parapsychology tries to establish the reality of and the explanation of foreknowledge, for example. But clearly parapsychology has come nowhere near such a breakthrough. Without this breakthrough, though, scrying continues to flounder, and we still lack an understanding of why this ancient trade has persisted for so long in human culture.

CHAPTER 5

SIX MONTHS SPENT AS A SCRYER

After all my research into the subject of scrying, what I still lacked was any real sense of what the day-to-day life of a practitioner would be like—what sort of person(s) present themselves to scryers and the questions these clients have for a seer. Accordingly, I decided to conduct a participant-observer exercise to gain insight(s) into these issues. I advertised my services as a crystal ball diviner by brochure and actually worked as one during a six-month period.

I attempted to make this situation as close to the original as possible, even going so far as to charge a fee ($75.00 for a one-hour session) feeling that it was only through actually receiving payment that I would be able to think of myself as engaging in this activity professionally.

My project was announced to my friends verbally, and word about the venture spread by word of mouth. Friends who had organized a conference on the paranormal at a college invited me to participate, not only as a lecturer, but also as one of the "psychics" who came to the event to hire themselves out for one-on-one consultations. Other clients came to see me at a special facility which I had developed for the study of altered states of consciousness. I saw a number of other clients at a bookstore and at a New Age conference center.

However, I could not in good conscience represent to clients that I had "psychic powers," since I have no opinion as to whether they even exist. I made it my practice to explain to each client at the beginning of his or her session that my activity was entirely limited to reporting the visions I saw in the crystal ball, that I was skeptical about psychic phenomena, and that in no way did I purport to interpret the visions which I saw in the ball. It would be up to the individual client to interpret the reported visions as she saw fit.

Even though I briefly flirted with the idea of adding some color and pizzazz to my role by bedizening myself in turban and robe, I couldn't bring myself to carry through with this in actual practice. Hence, my manner of proceeding was considerably tamer than what one might encounter upon consulting more conventional (or convincing) scryers.

Finally, I added a fifteen-minute prologue during which I outlined my notions about the nature of scrying to the client(s) and also informed them about crystal visions and other hypnagogic phenomena. I felt that to do so would add educational value to the encounter.

I conducted these scrying sessions for a total of fourteen clients, and in doing so, made a number of highly surprising discoveries. One was that, given the desire, I would have had little difficulty in actually making a living at this trade. As word got around, people were lining up for sessions! Another surprise was that generally my clients seemed eager to relate the visions I had to their life situations. For example, when I told one middle-aged man that I saw a huge ocean liner with icebergs in the background, he remarked that in fact he was soon going on an ocean voyage to England. When I said that I saw him as an adolescent boy sitting on a bed with a chenille bedspread in a room, the windows of which looked out onto an L-shaped wooden porch, he recognized this as his childhood home.

Another middle-aged man told me that my visions of a little gray dog with curly hair had to do with his little dog of the same description. And so on and on.

Almost every client had the impression that the stream of images which I described related, in some obvious way, to his present real-life situation and concerns. Throughout each encounter, I sensed how the client struggled to make sense of the image in relation to his life.

When I attended the college conference on the paranormal, some of the organizers administered questionnaires to everyone who had a session with one of the psychics. Imagine my astonishment when they informed me that I received far and away the highest rating of all the psychics present that day, all the rest of whom were professionals who claimed actually to possess paranormal abilities. I learned later that this fact had provoked quite a bit of consternation and anger among the others. It turned out that the power hierarchy among the psychics in that locality was a rigid matriarchy and that I had offended them by bypassing their informal organization.

It remains to be seen why it is that clients in that situation have the impression that the seer's visions bear a relation to the life of the client. It is entirely possible that the seer responds on an unconscious, or preconscious, level to the demeanor, body language, and personality of the client, and then projects this subconscious insight in the form of an eidetic vision incorporating that theme. Freud believed that this was one mechanism by which "fortune telling" took place and a few incidents which occurred during my study were suggestive in this regard.

For example, during a session with a young man in his mid-twenties, I saw a vision of him dressed in a white tunic practicing one of the martial arts, which turned out to be accurate. Upon reflection, I realized that I probably had subconsciously inferred this from his body habitus, plus the fact that I already knew that he was interested in New Age subjects.

Finally, it was through this participant-observer encounter that, I believe, I glimpsed the answer to the riddle of why the antique profession of scrying has persisted for so long, and perhaps why fringe professions, in general, continue throughout recorded history to cycle into and out of prominence. During my six months spent as a scryer, I came to realize that people who come to a fortune teller do so primarily as a way of seeking relief from anxiety.

I arrived at this judgment simply from talking with my clients about what led them to come to see me and by observing their responses to the sessions, but the principle seems helpful in understanding several features of scrying, and of fringe professions generally. It certainly sheds light on why fringe practitioners are so fond of authoritative pronouncements: it is a commonplace among psychotherapists that one can be most helpful to an anxious client by assuming a self-confident, assertive stance.

Anxious people cannot follow long, involved explanations, and typically have no use for them anyway when circumstances are pressing. Accordingly, among the fringe professions we tend to find either simplistic ideologies which are not very hard to grasp ("All disease is caused by poor nutrition," etc.) or else mysterious mumbo-jumbo, as with the scryer's rituals and exotic dress.

In the first case, the message to the client is that the theories of the profession are obvious and require no mental effort on the part of the client. In the second the message is that the client need not bother with the details anyway, because they are supernatural mysteries accessible only to gifted adepts and not to us mere mortals.

The analysis of the profession of scrying which has been given until now enables us to see how this activity has generated confusion, which has resulted in potentially important psychological phenomena being ignored by scholars. In the next section, I will close by attempting to dispel the very concept of scrying, a notion which hovers as a dark cloud over the proper study of certain altered states of consciousness which have been of historical significance.

CHAPTER 6

SCRYING: AN IMAGE TO BE OVERCOME

Scrying depends for its continued existence as an activity and as a trade on a complex, interwoven fabric of factors. The most obvious factor is that of all fringe professions: their ultimate aim (whether this be openly acknowledged, vehemently denied or only preconsciously sensed, whether by practitioner or client) is no more and no less than the alleviation of anxiety. Science, unlike such pseudo-professions, cannot condone simple answers simply for the sake of alleviation of anxiety, so there will always be fertile ground for the purveyors of simplistic answers and "certainty."

The profession of scrying itself, in collusion with the public perceptions and misperceptions of the trade, espouses and perpetuates the attitude that the scryer is one possessed of a strange and supernatural gift. Furthermore, in doing so it glosses over—indeed, fails to acknowledge—the fact that the supposed "gift" itself is ambiguous.

Do scryers hold that their gift consists of being able to *see* visions in a crystal ball, or of being able to *interpret* the visions so as to reveal the future, or both? I doubt that most would even be aware of the distinction, but whatever answer they give would result in major difficulties.

It is an established psychological fact that an appreciable proportion of the normal population possesses the ability to see visions in a clear depth, while the existence of a faculty of foreknowledge has not been confirmed by science and—some argue—is in principle not susceptible to rational confirmation or disconfirmation.

Science has attempted to deal with the continuing embarrassment which scrying and other forms of divination represent *vis a vis* the rational world view by ignoring it and by erecting a taboo in order to keep serious investigators away from the topic. A major difficulty with this approach, however, is that even if society were able to extinguish the practice of scrying, crystal visions would continue to occur and would continue to be re-discovered by individuals who are prone to such altered states of consciousness. Such individuals would continue, as they have repeatedly in the past, to devise pseudo-explanations of these phenomena along paranormal and precognitive lines, and the cycle would begin anew.

I submit that the most effective way of eliminating this atavistic practice would be to bring the human faculty of crystal visions out into the open and subject it to a thoroughgoing interdisciplinary analysis—psychological, electrophysiological, historical, and literary. It should be noted at this point that the continuation of scrying as an image is precisely the factor which has deterred such an extensive and systematic investigation.

Scrying depends for its genesis, its spread, and its continuation over time upon public ignorance about the subject of crystal visions. Were the public well-informed about the existence and the nature of crystal visions, scrying as a specialized trade might well disappear once and for all. People would very rapidly realize that no specialized or extraordinary gift is involved; that, in fact, many of us are able to experience crystal visions.

Scrying has been able to forestall public examination of its doctrine by pretending to a special gift or ability. The very implausibility of its claim to possess such a gift, coupled with the public perception that the whole thing is a superstition, has blinded serious investigators to a most interesting field of study, namely, crystal visions.

From this time forward, I propose, let us clearly distinguish the fact that crystal visions occur apart from their illicit and exploitative use by scryers—persons who pretend to be able to divine occult knowledge. In doing so, we will come to realize that in this, as in so many other instances, what at first appears paranormal can, upon analysis and reflection, be seen at long last to be quite normal.

What has gone before has been fairly abstract. Let us now apply all this by fleshing out this presentation with some particular examples.

PART II

HARUSPICY, MRS. BOLLSWORTH'S MOTHER'S MAID, THE INSTRUMENT OF ARTEPHIUS, AND OTHER CURIOSITIES OF LONG AGO

CHAPTER 1

THE INSTRUMENT OF ARTEPHIUS,
AND OTHER CURIOSITIES OF
LONG AGO

As we have seen, it is not possible to compose a proper history of scrying. Nonetheless, it is instructive to leaf through the pages of time to discover the strange art as it has popped up here and there, to reconstruct and to remember the lives of those people who were its practitioners.

But in order to put scrying into the proper light, I must adopt a style of presentation which is at variance with that found in the Thomas and Besterman books. By showing how they run aground, I hope to provide a remedy for the defects found in those two volumes. Both books are deficient in some of the same respects: Both fail miserably to differentiate between scrying and other uses to which crystal gazing has been or can be put. Both authors are so obsessed with the difficulties of demonstrating the paranormal (subspecies: divination) that they write in a way that obscures the fact that a demonstrable and fascinating psychological phenomenon (crystal visions) underlies the practice of scrying. Neither author has personal firsthand experience with crystal visions, so both books fail to convey an experiential feel for the subject. Consequently, they end up portraying scrying as a dry, antique curiosity rather than as a colorful, human reality. In the process, both bumble into the error of trying to compose a history of scrying; consequently, they both end up creating instead a colorless patchwork of anecdotes masquerading as a scholarly presentation.

Besterman makes a more scholarly display of the same error, since he puts the same kind of materials together in a more orderly structure than does Thomas, uses more footnotes and cites more references. He also includes an arrogant scholarly critique of Thomas's book, as I am now including of his and Thomas's. So both end up depriving scrying of its life and color, a misstep I would like to avoid.

However, because of the way these books were written, they can be mined for a wealth of anecdotes about scrying. These anecdotes can then be reassembled in such a way as to paint an impressionistic portrait of the phenomenon of scrying over time. This technique has the advantage of highlighting the inherent charm and interest of the anecdotes themselves.

Concurrently, particular points and observations about the practice of scrying can be made and illustrated by the anecdotes. Reading these anecdotes in the context of the knowledge about scrying set out in Part I, this style of presentation can cast light on particular curious episodes of history as if by a kind of flashbulb effect, capturing each in a freeze-frame of sudden illumination. In what follows, I include anecdotes drawn from Thomas and Besterman as well as similar anecdotes from other sources not specifically about scrying or crystal gazing.

CHAPTER 2

THE LIGHTNING-LEARNED LIVER LOOKERS

It is not known precisely where haruspicy, divination by inspecting the entrails of sacrificed animals, originated—perhaps in Babylon, perhaps in Greece. It is mentioned in *Ezekiel 21:21*,

> "For the king of Babylon halts to take
> the omens at the parting of the ways,
> where the road divides. He casts lots
> with arrows, consults teraphim and
> inspects the livers of beasts."

We do know, however, that the Romans received the art from the Etruscans. Even in the times of the Roman Empire, this mode of divination was the sole province, indeed the inherited prerogative and civic responsibility, of families of Etruscan lineage. These respected diviners exerted a strong political influence through their close connection with the aristocrats of Rome (just as psychics today flock around movie stars). A chair of haruspicy was maintained by the state in Rome, so as to insure a steady supply of these indispensable technicians. (It staggers the mind to try to imagine what their training institute was like.) Politicians and wealthy citizens hired their own personal haruspicers.

The haruspicers utilized an assortment of techniques, but the essential one was the art of divination through the inspection of the entrails of animals slaughtered for the purpose. In particular, they were most interested in the liver. It was primarily by the viewing of that organ that they deciphered the future. (The ancient Babylonians regarded the liver as the seat of the soul.)

As the centuries wore on, the prophecies of these functionaries began to take on a steadily more conservative bent. Eventually, there must have been rumblings in the Senate about taking these proud old families off the dole, for in the first century A.D. the Emperor Claudius felt obliged to speak up in their defense. Tacitus recorded Claudius's reflections as follows:

> "This oldest Italian art ought not to die out through neglect. The advice of soothsayers, consulted in time of disaster, has often caused the revival and more correct subsequent observance of religious ceremonies. Moreover, leading Etruscans, on their own initiative—or the Roman Senate's —have kept up the art and handed it down from father to son. Now, however, public indifference to praiseworthy accomplishments has caused its neglect; and the advance of foreign superstitions has contributed to this. At present all is well. But gratitude for divine favor must be shown by insuring that rites observed in bad times are not forgotten in prosperity (Tacitus *Annals 11.15*)."

One suspects that in its earliest appearance haruspicy was a variant of scrying. The liquid, reflective expanse of a freshly exposed liver could easily serve as a speculum. The general decline of the art may have been accompanied by a growing standardization of the procedure which would have taken place in the following way. The pioneers were, in fact, adept at entering into a visionary state through gazing into a clear depth. After they discovered this faculty, fortuitous coincidences, or sage, unconscious extrapolation, convinced them that the visions could be interpreted so as to foretell future events. The originators endeavored to pass along their skill to pupils. The trade proved to provide a good living, and also worked its way into the power structure as an occupation vital to national security.

Somewhere in the course of these developments, the clear-depth gazing itself was phased out. Perhaps so many aspirants were unable to see visions that they exerted pressure for a more analytical and left-brained approach. So a bump on that lobe at such-and-such a position was an omen of disaster, this shape of that edge of the liver meant a change of regimen, and so on. Indeed, models of livers—marked off in plots and sectors and covered with interpretative symbols—have been recovered. Obviously, these artifacts were teaching aids for the use of professors and students and practitioners of the trade. They were made of a variety of substances, among them bronze and alabaster. As time passed by, disillusionment with the trade developed into looming extinction. Augustus was a great fan of the haruspicers, but he forbade them to respond to inquiries about death.

Our knowledge about scrying can perhaps help clarify the origin of haruspicy, but, unfortunately, it sheds no light at all on one of the most colorful aspects of that intriguing antique profession. For the haruspicers were charged also with making for the public determinations of the messages brought by bolts of lightning. Whenever lightning struck, it was the duty of the liver diviners to hasten to the scene. They had to cleanse the spot, bury debris of the explosion, fence in the area and consecrate it to Jupiter with a commemorative plaque.

They determined the bolt's meaning, and the god from which it came, by the use of the manuals known as *The Lightning Books*. These books preserved and promulgated all the accumulated wisdom about lightning, along with recipes for expatiating it and instructions on how to investigate it. Surely it is one of the great tragedies of the study of divination that these volumes are now long lost to us.

Pope Innocent I, in desperation, briefly allowed them back from obscurity in 408 A.D., when the Etruscan haruspicers rashly promised him that they would save Rome by calling down the bolts against Alaric. So lightning was bound up, too, and was haruspicy's last hurrah.

CHAPTER 3

ROGER BACON'S MAGIC MIRROR

There are certain historical personages whose visages have become blurred, as it were, in our collective visions. They have come to inhabit a twilight zone of legend, a halfway house between merely folk-heros and flesh and blood reality. Roger Bacon is a good example.

Roger Bacon (1214-1292) was, indeed, an actual person, but some of the talents and discoveries which have come to be attributed to him seem impossible to believe. General knowledge about scrying can help us separate what is truth about this man (and others like him) from what is legend, what is plausible, and what is not plausible.

According to *The Famous History of Friar Bacon*, an old compendium of the legends that have grown up around him, Bacon made a magic mirror for remote viewing. The book relates that two young men who were close friends came to Bacon and asked him to let them look in the magic mirror to see what their fathers were doing at that moment in a distant place.

> "The fathers of these two gentlemen (in their sons' absence) had become great foes: this hatred between them was grown to that height, that wherever they met, that they had not only words, but blows. Just at that time, as it should seem, that their

41

sons were looking to see whether they were in good health, they had met and drawn and were at each others' ears. Their sons seeing this, and having always been great friends, didn't know what to say to one another, but beheld each other with angry looks. At last one of their fathers, as they might perceive in the glass, had a fall, and the other, taking advantage, stood over him ready to strike him. The son of the one that was down then could contain himself no longer but told the other young man, that his father had received wrong, but he answered that it was fair. At last there grew such foul words between them, and their bloods were so heated, that they presently stabbed each other with their daggers, and so fell down dead."

It is plausible to assume that Bacon could, indeed, have possessed a "magic mirror," and that two students could have possibly seen images such as are described. Coincidences which have occurred during my experimentation with crystal gazers make it plausible for me further to allow the possibility of the alleged veridicality of this collective vision. It is quite possible that unconscious awareness, on the part of the students, of subsurface tension between their fathers influenced the content of the vision. The students' reaction seems a predictable outcome to the joint vision, possibly deriving also from unconscious tension between the two of them. I conclude that this tale is plausible enough that no one can conclude from its content alone that the story is fictional.

CHAPTER 4

THE THREE VASES OF ARTEPHIUS

Emile Grillot de Givry, a European authority on witchcraft, uncovered the makings of a haunting tale indeed in an unpublished manuscript in the Bibliotheque de l'Arsenal. In Givry's *Illustrated Anthology of Sorcery, Magic and Alchemy*, (pp. 307-308), he relates some of what he found in the manuscript.

We come across a naive figure drawn in a rudimentary manner. At the foot of the drawing "the hill upon which one works" is represented. Higher up is the table on two trestles in a "solitary and fitting high place." It has to be enclosed in some sort of structure of which the author gives no explanation, but which he represents as being of "wood pierced all about with holes to receive the rays of the moon and stars." Upon the table are three vases, one of the earthenware, containing oil of myrrh, another of green earthenware, containing wine, and a third of white earthenware, containing water. The last two may be replaced by vases of copper and glass respectively. A cloth is placed on the vase of water, which has a lighted candle beside it; two or more of these stand in the spaces between the three vases. It seems that three instruments are necessary—a wand of poplar-wood, "half without bark," a bright knife, and a pumpkin-root; these are also shown in the drawing, but the author has unluckily forgotten to tell us their use.

He does, however, tell us that "Artephius made an instrument and prepared it with vases in this manner: by the earthenware vase is the past known, by the copper vase the present, and by the glass vase the future. He arranges them in yet another fashion; that is to say, in place of the earthenware vase a silver vase full of wine is set, and the copper one is filled with oil, and the glass with water. Then you will see present things in the earthen vase, past things in the copper, and future things in the silver...All must be shielded from the sun; and the weather must be very calm, and must have been so for at least three days. By day you will work in sunny weather, and by night in the moonlight and by the light of the stars. The work must be done in a place far from any noise, and all must be in deep silence. The operator is to be garbed all in white, and his head and face covered with a piece of red silken stuff or fine linen, so that nothing may be visible but the eyes...In the water the shadow of the thing is seen, in the oil the appearance of the person, and in the wine the very thing itself; and there is the end of this invention.

These words are from de Givry's classic, to which the reader is referred for the intriguing drawing mentioned in the quote, which constitutes a strangely alluring word picture of an early scryer's whimsical romantic attempt to standardize his pseudo-profession. It is worthwhile to note that, for a long period, science and magic were all mixed up, in the minds of laymen and learned alike. The stumbling attempts of alchemists and magicians, from time to time, resulted in replicable discoveries. Partly out of such a jumble, chemistry and other sciences, as we know them, emerged.

CHAPTER 5

HE EMPEROR AND THE HYDROMANCER

Scrying was known among the Romans. Northcote Thomas told a story he attributed to an ancient unnamed source, of how an emperor consulted a seer who told fortunes by gazing into water.

> Andronicus Comnenus had recourse to a hydromantic diviner to discover his successor, whom he intended to dispose of by violent means at the first opportunity. The water, as is sometimes the case with the crystal in the hands of present-day scryers, gave such messages as were vouchsafed mirrorwise—in other words, the letters S I, which formed the whole of the first answer, and were interpreted to mean Isaac Angelus, appeared in reverse order. The prediction was verified; but perhaps the scryer had a shrewd suspicion as to the probable course of events, for Comnenus was by no means popular.

Is it a property of the literary, or historical imagination, or a strange quirk of reality itself—or some unknown—that accounts for the tragic connection between politician and prophecy? Why are we so eager to entertain the possibility that someone foresaw Kennedy's assassination, or the old adage that Lincoln foresaw his own death? And why is it so irresistible to ask, "What if Caesar had listened to his seer?"

The Emperor Andronicus' plight reminds one, to a degree, of the original chronicle of the actual, flesh and blood, MacBeth (Makbeth), an account I find more bone-chilling than Shakespeare's tragic drama.

> And these were the wars that Duncane had with foreign enemies, in the seventh year of his reign. Shortly after happened a strange and uncouth wonder, which afterward was the cause of much trouble in the realm of Scotland, as ye shall after hear. It fortuned as Makbeth and Banquho journeyed towards Fores, where the king then lay, they went sporting by the way together without other company, save only themselves, passing through the woods and fields, when suddenly in the midst of a land, there met them three women in strange and wild apparel, resembling creatures of elder world, whom when they attentively beheld, wondering much at the sight, the first of them spoke and said: "All hail Makbeth, Thane of Glamis" (for he had lately entered into that dignity and office by the death of his father Sinell). The second of them said: "Hail Makbeth, Thane of Cawder." But the third said: "All hail Makbeth that hereafter shalt be king of Scotland."
>
> Then Banquho: "What manner of women (saith he) are you, that seem

so little favorable unto me, whereas to my fellow here, besides high offices, ye assign also the kingdom, appointing forth nothing for me at all?" "Yes (saith the first of them) we promise greater benefits unto thee, that unto him, for he shall reign indeed, but with an unlucky end: neither shall he leave any issue behind him to succeed in his place, where contrarily thou indeed shalt not reign at all, but of thee those shall be born which shall govern the Scottish kingdom by long order of continual descent."

Herewith the foresaid women vanished immediately out of their sight. This was reputed at the first but some vain fantastical illusion by Makbeth and Banquho, insomuch that Banquho would call Makbeth in jest, king of Scotland; and Makbeth again would call him in sport likewise, the father of many kings. But afterwards the common opinion was, that these women were either the weird sisters, that is (as ye would say) the goddesses of destiny, or else some nymphs or fairies, endued with knowledge of prophecy by their necromantic science, because everything came to pass as they had spoken. For shortly after, the Thane of Cawder being condemned at Fores of treason against the king committed; his lands, livings, and offices were given of the king's liberality to Makbeth.

There is an element of compelling fatality in tales of politicians and seers. The anecdote about Andronicus is a specimen attempt to explain the phenomenon in terms of the political savvy of the diviner.

The reported events of MacBeth's life suggest the possibility of fulfillment of the prophecy because of the subject's efforts to bring it about, as if in response to fate.

Accounts like these are used by devotees of the occult to establish the role of the paranormal in the lives of the powerful and by others to show how prophecy has its effect through human psychology.

CHAPTER 6

MYSTIC MAID

A manuscript written by W. Shippon and dated June 24, 1691, is preserved in the British Museum. It is a record of happenings related to the writer by a certain Mrs. Bollsworth. It is rendered here by me into contemporary English for the purpose of enhancing its readability while, hopefully, preserving its inherent charm.

Mrs. Bollsworth's mother had a maid whose name was Bess. When Bess's mistress was out, Bess was busy in an arbor in the garden where Mrs. Bollsworth, being then a girl, found Bess looking in a copper basin with water in it. The girl had heard that the maid was a witch and was curious to see this. The maid was unwilling, at first, but at last allowed Mrs. Bollsworth to look into the basin. Looking into it, she spied something through it, as though it had been a glass, and saw as if it were the shape of a great number of men fighting one with another which, after, was judged to be the representation of Worcester's fight, it being at that time. The maid told her mistress and all in the house the same night or day after it was fought, saying that the King's party was worsted, and told of several particulars of the fight, which she saw and learned in that basin.

A second trick of this maid, to which Mrs. Bollsworth was a witness, was her showing a gentleman his mistress in a common looking glass, putting behind it a paper with barbarous words and

51

characters on it. She bid the gentleman, and 2 or 3 more (among them Mrs. Bollsworth), to look in it and they all saw (as they said in Mrs. Bollsworth's hearing) and she particularly for herself averred that she saw a gentlewoman very distinctly in the glass in the daytime picking her teeth which the gentleman confessed was his very mistress. They desired the maid to show her again in the afternoon, which Mrs. Bollsworth and the rest saw again in another posture with a book in her hand and sitting in a coach. This gentleman, after asking his lady her postures and business those two times, confessed it was true what they saw.

A young woman, known in the family, desired Bess to show her her sweetheart, which she did in the looking glass, showing a man under the barber's hand, who starting up suddenly, his face seemed bloody. This Mrs. Bollsworth saw very plainly with the rest of the company: upon enquiry the gentleman was at that first time found to have been cut by a barber and rose up hastily. Mr. Bollsworth also heard the particulars of this same story from the said gentleman as well as from his wife 30 years ago...Mrs. Bollsworth saw several other times but less perfect shapes. Bess would let nobody stand behind the glass. Afterwards several people came to know their fortunes and find lost things.

What sort of group conscious (or unconscious) processes form the basis of collective scrying visions such as these? What was there about Bess—what factors of personality or talent, for example, that gave her the ability to unify this group of people so that they would collectively produce and experience these phenomena? If, in the future, widespread experimentation with crystal gazing takes place, possibly issues like these could be clarified.

CHAPTER 7.

THE PUNISHMENT FOR SCRYING

Today scrying is legally proscribed. In the days before the tyranny of religious authority was controlled by democratic change, scrying was classified as heresy. Out of its loving concern for humanity, the church, on many an occasion and with little excuse or evidence, burned these "dangerous" offenders at the stake.

Besterman recovered a startling memento for aspiring scryers from *The Archeological Journal* of 1856. He gives the details as follows:

> The earliest known document relating to scrying is the confession made by one William Byg, alias Lech, at Wombwell in Yorkshire, on the 22nd of August 1467. He had earned his livelihood for a year or two by finding stolen property through the aid of his crystal, but had eventually been charged with heresy, that portmanteau accusation. In his confession Byg describes the procedure he adopted when searching in the crystal for information; it does not differ in the least from that of later scryers. He employed a pure boy, made the usual invocations to the heavens and to all therein, and then addressed the boy (the only English in the document), "Say we trewe, chylde, what

man, what woman, or what childe hase stolen y thyng..." As punishment Byg had to walk at the head of a procession in the Cathedral Church of York with a lighted torch in his right hand and his books depending from a stick in his left; three placards were to be fixed on him: one on his head with the words "Ecce sortilegus," one on his breast inscribed "Invocator Spirituum," and one on his back bearing the solitary, dread "Sortilegus." He had to make a full recantation and to burn his books, the recantation to be repeated in the parish churches of Pontefract, Barnsley, Doncaster, and Rotherham. Byg was no doubt thankful to get off so lightly.

Even today, persons involved in investigating scrying would probably be set upon by religious fundamentalists who would charge them with aiding and abetting Satan, or with condoning, or practicing, witchcraft or Satanism.

What is the basis of the fundamentalist's obsession with ideas of lurking demons? Are they avoiding confronting the dark sides of themselves? To what degree do their ideological preoccupation and their focus upon cognition (*i.e.* belief) as the essence of religion reflect obsessive-compulsive concerns?

These issues are of growing concern not only *vis a vis* the study of the paranormal, but in the larger social and political arenas. Religious fundamentalists are now attempting to set the agenda for the rest of us in many important departments of our lives; they seem to be suffering under the delusion that they can obtain the inner security they subconsciously long for by enforcing ideological conformity on the rest of us.

The systematic study of scrying should give us an excellent field to scrutinize the general problem of fundamentalism in a microcosmic context.

PART III

CHAPTER 1

MUMBO-JUMBO:
LEVELS AND FUNCTIONS OF
RITUALS IN SCRYING

Scrying is surrounded, and perhaps encumbered, by rituals and ceremonies in historical anecdote, in public perception, and in actual practice.

According to Andrew Lang, "The magical ceremonies, which probably have nothing to do with the matter, have succeeded in making this old and nearly universal belief seem a mere fantastic superstition."

It may be impossible, or at least undesirable, entirely to eliminate mumbo-jumbo from the study of scrying. However, as a workbook task, the reader now must consider a list of eight kinds of ritualistic, or ceremonial, practices that I have been able so far to delineate in the course of much research into, and thinking about, the subject of scrying. The reader is invited to add others of his own, or to make further distinctions, and all of this is for the purpose of bringing to awareness aspects of the practice that must be taken into account in conducting a study of scrying.

Here, then, are the types of scrying rituals that I have been able to discern, along with their functions.

(1) *Induction Rituals* - facilitate the scryer's entrance into the hypnagogic state.

59

(2) *Context or Boundary Rituals* - serve to establish or define the relationship between the scryer and her client.

(3) *Protection Rituals* - overtly they are said to be for the purpose of warding off evil spirits, but they have the intrapsychic purpose of preventing the eruption of supposedly overwhelming or threatening contents from the unconscious to the conscious mind.

(4) *Initiation Rituals* - serve to ease the client into a state of receptiveness to the scryer's pronouncements.

(5) *Selection Rituals* - serve as guidelines for choosing a surrogate gazer, when the scryer interprets the invoked crystal visions of another person.

(6) *Framing Rituals* - consists of the questions addressed by the process; in effect, directions to the unconscious as to what images to allow to flow into the conscious mind, and instructions as to how those images are to be interpreted.

(7) Interpretation Rules - rules, which may be cataloged, for example, in presentation, which specify how particular images are to be interpreted.

(8) Acquisition/Preparation Rules - guidelines whereby the speculum is to be acquired and/or prepared by the gazer.

The reader is now invited to peruse both the Thomas book and the Besterman book and whatever other sources on scrying he may find, and to list all the examples of each kind of ritual he can discover there, along with a brief account of the basis for the identification.

The lists of all participants can be read and discussed in a group exercise. Let us specify that one ritual may, in fact, be included in a number of categories, and that my list of categories is not suggested to be a final or exhaustive one. Rather, it is intended to be the basis for beginning a discussion of ritual in scrying, a discussion that is to take place among participants in a proposed study, as follows.

PART IV
INITIAL DESCRIPTION OF A PROPOSED PROCEDURE FOR AN EXPERIENTIAL PARTICIPANT-OBSERVER EXERCISE FOR THE STUDY OF SCRYING

CHAPTER 1.

Procedure

Each of us who participates in this study is to be personally familiar, from firsthand experience, with the art of crystal gazing, in essence, a person highly gifted like so many others with the ability to see crystal visions.

Let each participant set up her own scrying parlor, where she is to pursue the trade of a scryer. Let each of us do it up right: let each studio be elaborately and exotically decorated; let the crystal ball or other speculum there displayed be beautiful and intriguing indeed. And let each participant bedizen herself in garments grand and magnificent. Let each participant conduct the practice as if her livelihood depended upon it; so let each of us charge a reasonable rate for our time.

Let us modify our practice in this way, however, from the actual trade of the scryer as it occurs normally: Let us all inform our clients fully that we will confine ourselves to the reporting of the visions we see on their behalf, as it were, in the crystal or other speculum, and will studiously refrain from interpreting the visions so seen in a paranormal direction.

Instead of claims as to what the future will bring, let us offer each client education. I suggest that, as in my pilot study for this project, mentioned in Part I, each session begin with a get-acquainted encounter and a thorough education session about the historical and psychological aspects of scrying. I further propose that the scrying session itself be followed by a discussion with the client in order to gauge his reactions to the procedure, to answer his questions, and to learn more ourselves about this fascinating old practice.

I further suggest that no one undertake this activity outside of a collective study group of scholars, or those who have a serious interest such as this book is attempting to enlist and organize. Finally, I hereby propose the above guidelines as a basis for beginning a discussion of what the further guidelines of this project are finally to be.

I believe that by undertaking such a project, and by maintaining regular consultation and discussion and interaction as we proceed, by forming a professional society of scholars of scrying, we stand to gain a great deal of understanding about the archetype of the seer. In effect, our activity will be at once a conceptual, educational and experiential enterprise, enabling us all to enrich our understanding of a primeval, shamanic modality through a firsthand encounter, a collective re-creation of an ancient and forgotten human tradition.

CHAPTER 2.

EXPERIENTIAL EXERCISE

For this next step, I don't recommend crystal balls for several reasons. They are more expensive than necessary, and even a five inch diameter glass ball may cost as much as one hundred dollars. They evoke associations, even if preconsciously, with superstition, because of their use in fortune telling. Most importantly, they focus the rays of the sun and can cause fires.

You can purchase an almost spherical glass fishbowl at most large retail stores. Then get a sturdy stand capable of holding the bowl, a strong metal tripod, for example. Place a strong, high table or plant stand at one end of the room, a few inches from a blank wall. Place the tripod on the tabletop.

Purchase about three yards of fine black or dark blue velvet. Drape it over the tripod and table with the velvety side up. Using transparent tape, secure the upper edge of the velvet to the wall about three feet above the tabletop and let the bottom edge of the cloth hang down in front of the table.

Then fill the fishbowl with water and carefully nestle it securely in the tripod through the cloth, *i.e.*, with the velvet between the bowl and the tripod. Check to make sure that the whole arrangement is stable and secure.

Making sure not to trip on the cloth, place a very comfortable chair about three feet in front of the table so that you can gaze into the bowl from about eye level or even a couple of inches below, *i.e.*, looking slightly upwards. Arrange all this so that you can relax your whole body and can lean your head comfortably back on the head rest of the chair when you are gazing into the bowl.

Candles, or small wattage light bulbs such as night lights, are probably the best light source for this exercise. However, be extremely careful with your candles and don't let them get anywhere near the cloth or other flammable objects or substances. Glass hurricane lamps or other devices can help prevent the candle flames from starting fires.

You will simply have to experiment in order to determine what the optimal light level is for you, but always place the candles at a distance behind the chair or at other locations around the room so that the flames will not create distracting reflections in the speculum.

Once the environment and the speculum are prepared, set aside a certain time, perhaps during the evening, for gazing. If your health permits, get some moderate exercise during the day before gazing, since this promotes deep muscle relaxation.

At the appointed time, check again to make sure your speculum is stable and secure, light the candles, turn out all other lights in the room, sit down in the chair, and sink into a deep state of relaxation. Without focusing, gaze through the water as if you were looking at something at a great distance. Don't try to force the visions, which are not under volitional control anyway, but rather assume an attitude of confident expectation that they will appear.

Don't pay any attention to the passage of time; don't look at a clock or your watch. Just rest there gazing, for as long as you are comfortable doing so. You may at first see clouds or colors moving by in the speculum before the vision show begins. Then the images begin to form in the speculum and play themselves out.

If nothing happens, don't worry. Just try again a couple of days later. Even if you never see anything in the speculum after several attempts, you may still be able to experience visions with the help of a guide.

Also, many therapists will be aware of techniques for helping you relax, which may help initiate crystal visions.

Keep a notebook for recording your visions after each gazing session. As you look back over notes from several gazing periods during a span of weeks, you may be surprised by how much you realize about yourself and your concerns. It may also be helpful for you to discuss your visions with another person, a trusted loved one or supportive friend who understands you very well.

Oddly, in our age this venerable art has been almost completely forgotten, surviving primarily as an object of ridicule in imaginative cartoons. However, recent psychological research has established beyond question that a real phenomenon lies at the heart of scrying, and that this technique can be taught and learned. Quite apart from speculations about fortune telling, crystal gazing has demonstrable benefits. It enables us to participate in and to personally understand the exotic world of the ancient visionaries and prophets who used it. Also, it is an excellent method for exploring the hidden realms of our own consciousness and for unleashing one's creative potential.

In an effort to better understand this phenomenon, and to compile data related to scrying, we would like to hear about the results of your experiments in scrying/crystal gazing. If you would like to share this information with me, please send a brief description of your experiment(s), and the results, to me in care of my publisher, R. Bemis Publishing, Ltd.; Post Office Box 71088; Marietta, Georgia 30007-1088.